Arms & Armour

Frederick Wilkinson

Macdonald Educational

Editor Anne Furniss
Design Peter Benoist
Production Philip Hughes
Picture Research Lorna Collin

First published 1975
Reprinted 1980

Macdonald Educational
Holywell House
Worship Street
London EC2A 2EN

contents

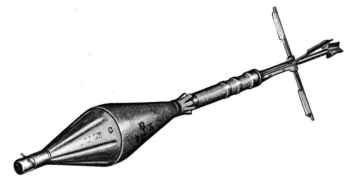

ISBN 0356 05092 0

Printed and bound by
New Interlitho, Milan, Italy

Primitive arms flint and metal

Core and flake weapons

Primitive man was always in danger and he had little with which to defend himself. He had to arm himself with weapons and the first were probably sticks and stones picked up from the ground. He discovered that when one kind of stone was broken the pieces had very sharp edges. He began to shape these pieces of stone and produced the first flint weapons and tools.

Flint is found in small blocks and if hit in a certain way it breaks off in flakes. These flakes can be chipped and shaped for use as arrow heads, spear heads and knife blades. The piece left over, the core, was shaped and used for axe heads and other tools.

The flint workers or knappers became very skilled but flint has several disadvantages which cannot be overcome. It breaks easily and it cannot be made into long, thin strips for blades.

The first metals

Someone discovered that if some types of rock were heated a liquid appeared which set hard when cold. Copper was the first metal to be discovered and for a time it was used to make weapons, but it is very soft.

If a little tin is mixed with copper the mixture, bronze, is much tougher. Metal smiths learned how to make moulds and pour in the molten metal and were able to make daggers, swords, axes, spear heads and shields.

Flint is found in nearly every part of the world. It is found lying on the surface and buried in layers underground. The flint makers or knappers became expert at shaping and polishing the stone. By the end of the New Stone Age the implements were finely shaped and beautifully polished.

▲ The pieces of flint were shaped in many ways. If the block was hit at certain points, flakes broke off. The core of the block was used to make axe heads or spear heads. The flakes were shaped and sharpened by pressure flaking, which broke small flakes from the edges.

▲ Edges were sharpened by pressing hard enough to break off tiny flakes. But not even a skilled knapper could fashion very long, thin blades of flint. They always broke when hit on the side. Metal blades were stronger.

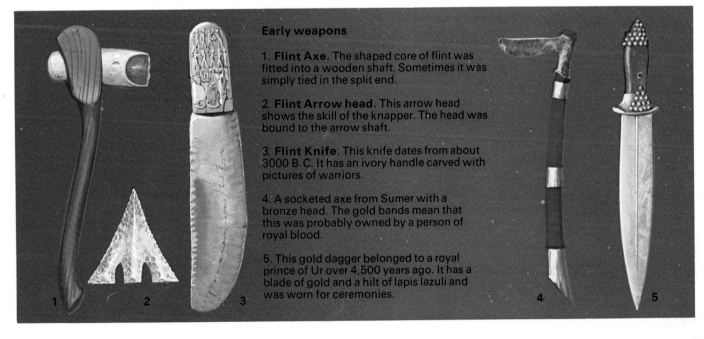

Early weapons

1. **Flint Axe.** The shaped core of flint was fitted into a wooden shaft. Sometimes it was simply tied in the split end.

2. **Flint Arrow head.** This arrow head shows the skill of the knapper. The head was bound to the arrow shaft.

3. **Flint Knife.** This knife dates from about 3000 B.C. It has an ivory handle carved with pictures of warriors.

4. A socketed axe from Sumer with a bronze head. The gold bands mean that this was probably owned by a person of royal blood.

5. This gold dagger belonged to a royal prince of Ur over 4,500 years ago. It has a blade of gold and a hilt of lapis lazuli and was worn for ceremonies.

Egyptians and Assyrians the first armies

The composite bow

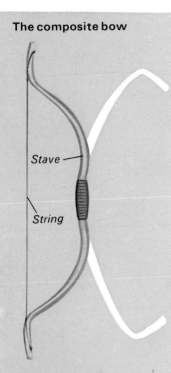

Stave

String

▲ Some Egyptian bows were wooden but others were made up of layers of wood, horn and sinew glued together. This construction gives a very springy stave which is very powerful. Without the string the stave bends almost into a circle.

▲ It requires great strength to string a composite bow because they are so springy. The archer placed his knee against the stave and held one end steady as he bent the other end around to meet the string.

▲ War chariots were developed about 3000 B.C. At first they were heavy and rather slow but the Egyptians developed a light, two-wheeled one. This painting shows a Pharaoh charging his enemies. The reins are tied around his waist to leave his hands free for the bow.

▼ The Assyrian army was very well organized. There were groups of mounted archers and heavy chariots carrying several warriors. The foot soldiers were divided into troops of slingers, spearmen and light and heavy archers protected by men carrying shields.

Shields and armour

Civilization began to develop in Egypt. Towns grew up and soon the country was ruled by a Pharaoh. In time he needed an army, so men were trained to fight together in large units. Most Egyptian troops carried a long spear but wore no armour. For protection they had large shields made of plaited reed or wood covered with leather.

Charioteers and archers wore armour, so they did not need a shield. This left their hands free to use weapons. Infantry weapons were mostly made of bronze and included swords and axes of various shapes.

A race of warriors

The Assyrians delighted in war and fought with all their neighbours. They trained and organized their armies well. They formed their infantry in bands of slingers, archers, spearmen and siege experts.

The Assyrian cavalry consisted of mounted archers and chariots which were slow but big enough to carry several archers and soldiers. They had troops specially trained for attacking walled cities and a number of large machines for making gaps in the walls.

When the Assyrian army crossed a river, the chariots were ferried over in boats whilst the troops swam or floated over on inflated animal skins.

Most Assyrian soldiers wore metal helmets which often had crests fixed on top. Their bodies were protected by long tunics covered with small overlapping scales made of bronze.

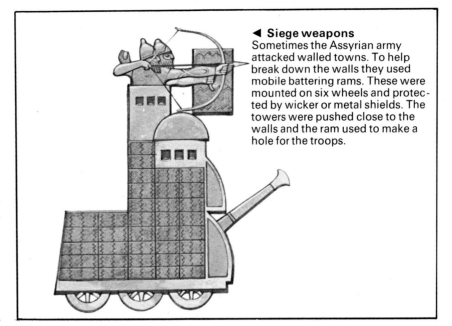

◄ Siege weapons
Sometimes the Assyrian army attacked walled towns. To help break down the walls they used mobile battering rams. These were mounted on six wheels and protected by wicker or metal shields. The towers were pushed close to the walls and the ram used to make a hole for the troops.

▼ Assyrian archer and shield bearer
Sometimes archers had to work very close to the enemy. They were then guarded by bearers carrying wicker shields.

▼ The army had many archers who used powerful composite bows. They wore long coats of bronze scale armour, a helmet and carried a short sword.

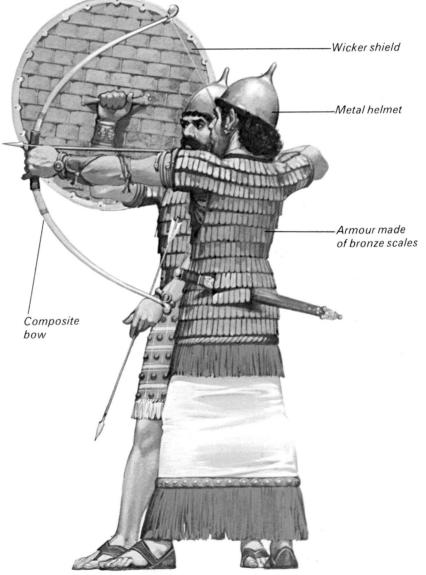

Wicker shield

Metal helmet

Armour made of bronze scales

Composite bow

The Greeks warriors of bronze

Greek phalanx

▲ The Greeks developed the phalanx, which was a kind of human battering ram. Lines of men equipped with a great shield, a sword and a long spear were formed into large groups.

Protected by their shields and with their spears at the ready, they slowly pressed forward until the enemy line broke or the phalanx was scattered.

Contests between champions

Ancient Greece was split into a number of small city states which were often at war with each other. They were also in constant danger of an attack from Persia, so the Greek armies were always well equipped.

The early Greek wars were often decided by individual combats. Much is known about these contests because Homer, a famous poet of Ancient Greece, wrote a poem about the siege of Troy.

Homer tells how the great heroes cast spears at each other and how they used their shields to protect themselves. When their spears of ash with bronze heads were broken or lost they fought with swords. Bows and arrows and chariots also played their part in these struggles. The warriors wore finely made armour and helmets of bronze, often with great crests on top.

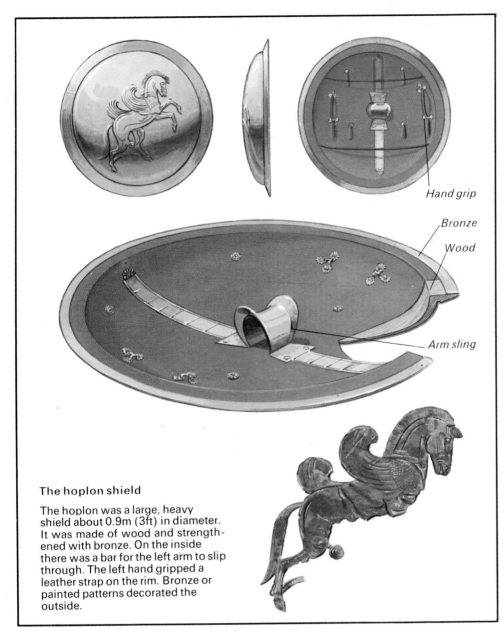

Hand grip

Bronze

Wood

Arm sling

The hoplon shield

The hoplon was a large, heavy shield about 0.9m (3ft) in diameter. It was made of wood and strengthened with bronze. On the inside there was a bar for the left arm to slip through. The left hand gripped a leather strap on the rim. Bronze or painted patterns decorated the outside.

▲ The Corinthian helmet was worn by many hoplites and covered the entire head. The face was guarded from slashes by the bar which projected down over the opening for the face.

▲ The Chalcidian helmet was smaller and lighter than the Corinthian helmet. The sides were less heavy and the wearer was able to hear through openings over the ears.

▲ The Boeotian helmet had a wide brim which protected the head but did not stop the wearer from being able to see all around him. It was worn by many cavalrymen.

The Phalanx

In the seventh century B.C. the old style of individual combat was replaced by the phalanx. This was a great block of lines of men called hoplites. They took their name from the great shield they carried, the hoplon. Each man was protected by his own shield and that of his neighbour. The hoplites were heavily armed, but relied on their long spears for attack.

Battles were fought on flat ground and were little more than pushing matches between the two sides. If the phalanx broke, the men were in great danger from the enemy cavalry, their archers and slingers.

During the Greek wars, the states often employed bands of soldiers called mercenaries who were not citizens but fought for anybody who would pay them. Some were archers from Crete, others were slingers from Rhodes.

Armour and weapons

The Greeks were master craftsmen and produced some beautifully made armour and weapons of bronze. The body was protected by a cuirass made up of a breast and back plate. These were made to fit comfortably but the breastplate was thicker to give greater protection. The lower part of the leg was protected by metal pieces called greaves and the hoplite had his great shield.

The hoplite carried a fairly short, slightly curved sword which had the cutting edge on the inside of the curve. The blade widened near the point.

Archers used some composite bows which were very curved and they carried about 24 arrows in a quiver. Throwing spears, or javelins, were used because they were heavy enough to pierce the armour. Some chariots were used but few cavalry.

7

The Roman legions

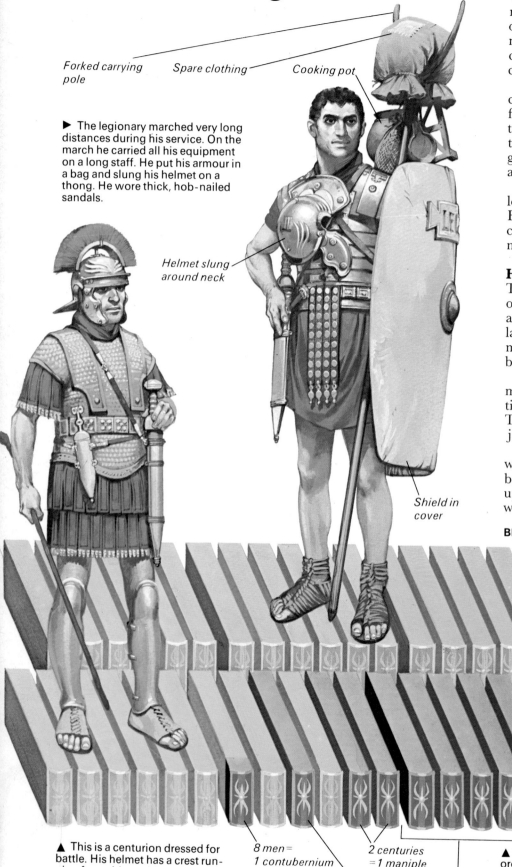

Forked carrying pole

Spare clothing

Cooking pot

▶ The legionary marched very long distances during his service. On the march he carried all his equipment on a long staff. He put his armour in a bag and slung his helmet on a thong. He wore thick, hob-nailed sandals.

Helmet slung around neck

Shield in cover

The greater part of Rome's army was made up of foot soldiers. They were organized into about 30 legions of 5,000 men. Only a Roman citizen could become a legionary, but the army also contained auxiliary troops.

Each legion was made up of ten cohorts and each of these, except the first cohort, was divided into six centuries. The first cohort had ten centuries. The centuries were split up into groups of eight men. Each group, called a contubernium, lived in one tent.

The legion was commanded by a legatus and under him were six tribunes. Each century was under the control of a centurion who had a second-in-command called an optio.

Hard training

The legionary wore a helmet of bronze or iron and was well protected by body armour called a lorica. He carried a large rectangular shield called a scutum, made of wood, leather and iron or bronze.

Training was hard and included marches and drill. The men had to practise for hours with swords and shields. They also learned to use the pilum, a javelin about 1.8 m. (6 ft) long.

One of the most important legionaries was the aquilifer, the chief standard bearer. The loss of a standard was looked upon as a terrible disgrace. The aquilifer wore a bearskin as part of his uniform.

Block diagram to show a legion on parade

▲ This is a centurion dressed for battle. His helmet has a crest running from side to side and his armour is of mail. Unlike the legionary, he has greaves to protect his legs. All centurions carried a wooden staff.

8 men = 1 contubernium

10 contubernia = 1 century

2 centuries = 1 maniple

6 centuries = 1 cohort

10 cohorts = 1 legion

▲ The Roman legion was a very well-organized fighting force. The 5,000 men were divided into ten cohorts, each of which were divided into centuries. Within each century, the men were organized in groups of eight men who worked and lived together.

▲ Legionaries were taught to fight in a set pattern. They carried two javelins and a short sword. The javelin, or pilum, had a long soft point which bent on impact, making movement difficult. The legionary threw his javelins first and then moved in with his sword drawn.

► Although some auxiliaries served in the infantry, many became cavalry men. They had two-edged swords which they used for slashing. Their shields were round or oval and they wore less armour than the legionary.

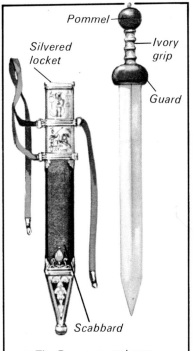

Pommel

Silvered locket

Ivory grip

Guard

Scabbard

▲ The Roman sword was short with a wide blade and called a gladius. Unlike most swords of the time it was used for stabbing and not for cutting. Some, like this one, were finely decorated. The gladius was carried on the right hand side and was drawn by tilting the hilt.

▲ On parade, the legion formed up in a slight semi-circle. The troops were formed in lines in a special order and the cohorts were arranged in two rows. Those containing the best men were placed on either flank and in the centre, whilst the weak cohorts were placed between them.

Mounted men in mail

▼ From Norway and Sweden the Vikings set out on their journeys to raid all the countries of Europe. Protected by their coats of mail, metal helmets and round wooden shields they spread terror wherever they went. When their longships beached they rounded up horses in order to travel long distances, but they preferred to fight on foot.

Raiding parties

The Romans had relied heavily on masses of well trained foot soldiers. After the collapse of their empire there was a change towards the use of mounted troops.

For centuries, parts of Europe were at the mercy of raiding parties of fierce mounted warriors. Some of these raiders, such as the Vikings, settled in the lands they conquered. In France they became the Normans and developed into very fierce cavalrymen.

The first knights

The Norman knight wore a hauberk, which was a coat of mail reaching to the knees and with sleeves to the elbow. The hauberk was split up the back and front so that the wearer could sit in his saddle. Mail was sometimes worn on the legs as well but most knights wore a coif, a hood of mail, to protect the head and neck. Beneath the hauberk the knight usually had some kind of padded garment which gave him extra protection and prevented the links rubbing his skin.

The Norman carried a big shield which was kite-shaped in order to cover his body from shoulder to foot as he sat in the saddle. He fought with sword, mace and lance. When the Normans charged their enemies they either tucked their lances under their arms or used them above their heads as stabbing weapons.

▲ Stirrups greatly increased the power of a mounted soldier. Without them he had to grip the sides of the horse with his knees to stay in the saddle. The stirrups enabled him to keep his legs straight and use the entire weight and power of his body for fighting.

How mail was made

▼ Mail is a very efficient form of armour but it is difficult to make. Lengths of thick iron wire were wound around a wooden or metal former and then cut into open rings. The ends of the rings were flattened and pierced with holes. Each ring was linked with four others and then the flat ends were overlapped and rivetted together.

Former

Chisel

Iron wire

Rivets

Ends flattened and rivetted

A Norman knight armed for battle

▶ The Norman knight was well protected by his hauberk, a long coat of mail. Over his head he wore a mail hood or coif and over this a conical helmet. His face was guarded by the nasal, a broad bar projecting from the rim of the helmet. He carried a long, kite shaped shield.

Spear

Helmet

Nasal

Coif

Shield

Hauberk

Sword tucked through hauberk

Padded under-garment

Spur

▲ The Bayeux Tapestry was made to commemorate the Battle of Hastings in 1066. On the far left is Odo, Duke William's brother. Even though he was a bishop he still took part in the battle, but he used a mace instead of a sword.

▲ It was difficult to recognise the Norman knights in their helmets with nasal bars. During the battle there was a rumour that Duke William had been killed. He raised his helmet to show himself to his followers.

▲ The Normans made great use of archers in all their battles. They used short bows and carried their arrows in quivers on their backs. Some wore mail hauberks like the knights, but many of them had no armour at all.

Mediaeval siege

▶ Defending the castle. It was most important to keep the enemy outside the walls. Mines were very dangerous and the defenders had to listen for the sounds of digging. If they heard the miners at work they dug a counter-mine, found the other tunnel and tried to drive out the attackers.

Ladders were pushed away from the walls by means of long poles. It was impossible to push over a siege tower and often the only way to deal with them and large catapults was to attack them. There was usually a small gate in the castle wall known as a sally port through which the attacking party could creep out.

A besieged castle in the 13th century

▲ A very successful method of breaching a castle wall was the mine. A tunnel was dug until it reached the stone foundations of the wall. The stones were removed and the space was filled with wood and inflammable material. When this was set on fire there was nothing to support the wall and it collapsed, leaving an opening for the attackers.

▲ Another useful weapon for the attack was the battering ram. It was usually mounted on a strong frame covered with a wooden roof. This was to protect the men using the ram. The heavy log was swung to and fro against one spot on the wall until it cracked.

Towers of strength

Castles played an important part in the Middle Ages. The site was carefully chosen to make it difficult for attackers. At first the castles were of wood but soon this was replaced by stone for greater strength.

Many castles were surrounded by a moat which was often filled with water. The walls were high with battlements at the top. The gateway was guarded with towers, a drawbridge and a portcullis.

A number of small towers were spaced around the walls to give archers the chance to fire along the walls without being in danger. Somewhere inside the walls was the strongest tower of all, the keep. Even if the attackers got into the castle the keep was strong enough to hold out on its own.

Siege tactics

When there was danger of attack, a castle would take in as many supplies as it could and close all its gates. The attackers would take up positions all around the castle to prevent any help getting in or anybody escaping.

Next they would examine the castle, looking for any weak places in the defences. When they had decided on their plan, the carpenters started to build the siege engines. To break the walls they had battering rams, catapults and trebuchets or they could use a mine.

If progress was slow they might decide to attack the walls. False attacks would be made to confuse the defenders and then the main assault would start. Parts of the moat were filled in with rocks, earth and trees and siege towers and ladders were pushed up to the walls. All the time the archers would keep up a constant rain of arrows.

If all the attacks were beaten back, the castle might have to be starved into surrender. This might take weeks or even years. Often the two commanders would arrange a meeting and agree that if help had not reached the castle by a certain date then it would surrender.

◀ During an attack on the castle walls, part of the moat was filled in. A tall wooden siege tower was pushed over the moat against the wall. At the top was a drawbridge which was let down on top of the wall. Wet skins protected the tower from fire.

▶ When a siege began, one of the first jobs was to build siege engines. The trebuchet was a large catapult worked by weights. The weights made a long arm swing over and hurl a large stone at the walls to break open a hole.

◀ Archers kept up a steady flow of arrows during an attack to make the defenders stay under cover. If the archer was in a position close to the castle walls he was protected by a large wooden shield called a pavise.

▶ The catapult was also used to batter holes in the wall. It was driven by the power of a great bunch of twisted ropes. The arm was pulled back and a stone put at the end. The arm was then freed and flew forward to throw the stone.

The change from links to plate

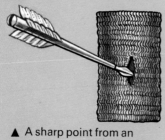

▲ A sharp point from an arrow, spear or sword could pierce the mail links.

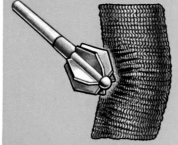

▲ Even if a weapon did not penetrate the mail it could still cause an injury.

Increased protection

Mail was a very good defence against most weapons. It would stop a sword, although the force of the blow would bruise the skin. Beneath the mail most knights wore a thick, padded garment and this helped soften any blows.

Mail was less satisfactory against sharp points. An arrow, a spear or a sword thrust might easily break through the links to cause a serious wound. To strengthen the mail the links could be made thicker, but this meant that it became heavier and stiffer.

Men began to wear more mail armour. Sleeves were extended to cover the hands and mail stockings were introduced to guard the legs. The coif covered more of the face and head.

This was still not enough, however. Knights demanded more protection, so armourers fitted pieces of metal to the mail. The first pieces were at the knees and the elbows and these were followed by other simple plates covering arms and legs.

The helmet was also improved to give greater defence. The nasal and neck guards were made bigger and soon the helmet completely covered the head except for slits in front of the eyes. It was known as the great helm.

The growth of heraldry

Armour covered more and more of the body and this made it much more difficult to recognize the wearer. In battle there was no time for doubt; there had to be an easy way to know a friend or an enemy. Knights began by using any badge but gradually a system known as heraldry grew up.

Important families took their own sets of colours and patterns called a coat of arms. They wore them on their surcoats, their shields and on the coverings of the horses. Often a model of part of the arms was fitted on top of the helmet. This was called the crest.

A College of Heralds was set up to control all matters concerning heraldry and to settle any quarrels. A special language to describe, or blazon, a coat of arms grew up.

Brasses and effigies

Much of our knowledge of armour and heraldry comes from brasses. These were placed in churches over the grave and showed the knight in his armour. Sometimes pieces of the knight's armour were hung above his tomb together with his sword. Later full size models of the knight were made and placed on top of the tomb instead of the brass.

The development of the great helm

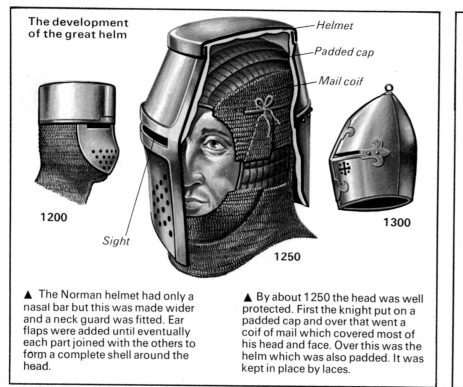

Helmet
Padded cap
Mail coif

1200
Sight
1250
1300

▲ The Norman helmet had only a nasal bar but this was made wider and a neck guard was fitted. Ear flaps were added until eventually each part joined with the others to form a complete shell around the head.

▲ By about 1250 the head was well protected. First the knight put on a padded cap and over that went a coif of mail which covered most of his head and face. Over this was the helm which was also padded. It was kept in place by laces.

Lord Scrope of Bolton

Lord Nevile of Raby

Bend

Saltire

Early examples of shields of arms

Heraldry was fairly simple at first but it soon began to build up its own rules and language. It became very complicated and each shape now has its own name.

The colours also have names, for instance red is called gules and black is sable. There were strict rules for describing or blazoning a coat of arms.

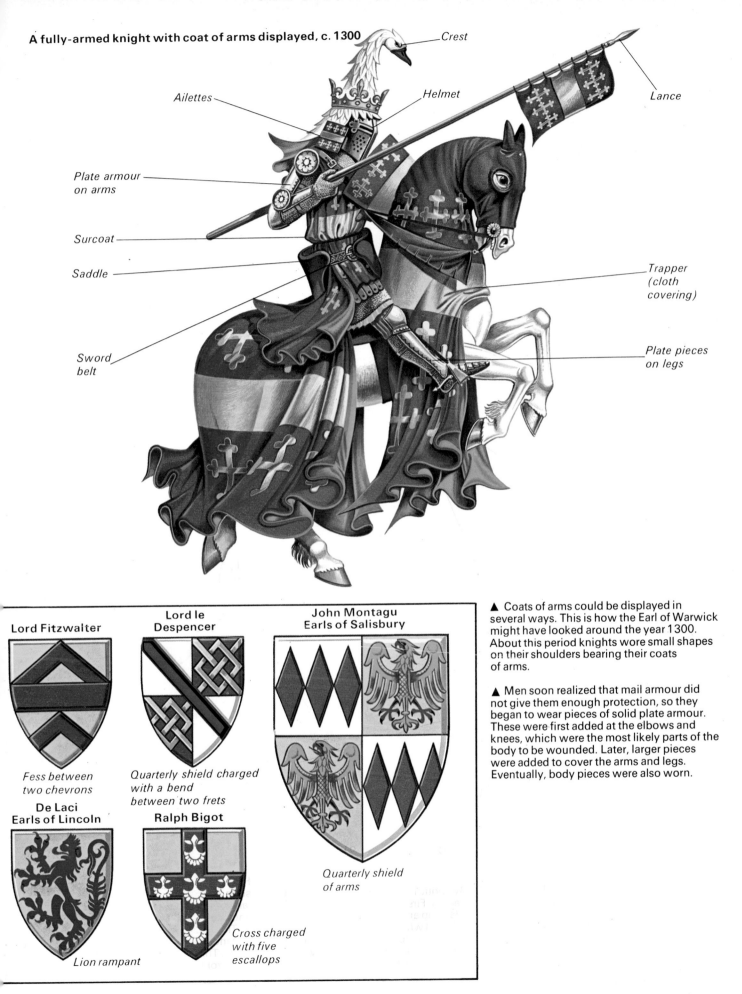

A fully-armed knight with coat of arms displayed, c. 1300

Crest

Ailettes

Helmet

Lance

Plate armour on arms

Surcoat

Saddle

Trapper (cloth covering)

Sword belt

Plate pieces on legs

Lord Fitzwalter

Fess between two chevrons

Lord le Despencer

Quarterly shield charged with a bend between two frets

John Montagu Earls of Salisbury

Quarterly shield of arms

De Laci Earls of Lincoln

Lion rampant

Ralph Bigot

Cross charged with five escallops

▲ Coats of arms could be displayed in several ways. This is how the Earl of Warwick might have looked around the year 1300. About this period knights wore small shapes on their shoulders bearing their coats of arms.

▲ Men soon realized that mail armour did not give them enough protection, so they began to wear pieces of solid plate armour. These were first added at the elbows and knees, which were the most likely parts of the body to be wounded. Later, larger pieces were added to cover the arms and legs. Eventually, body pieces were also worn.

The flight of arrows longbow and crossbow

▼ The English archer carried his longbow, spare string and wax for the string. His arrows were usually stored in a wagon until just before the battle. He often stuck them into the ground just in front of him so that he could grab them quickly and keep up a steady shower of arrows on the enemy.

How the longbow was made

◄ Yew was considered the best wood for making the longbow. The area of the tree trunk was carefully chosen so that the stave incorporated the strong older wood from the outside of the tree and the young, springy wood from inside.

Heart   Bark

► The bow staff was about 1.8 m. (6 ft) long and tapered from the centre towards each end. It was quite rough with notches at the end to hold the loops of the string.

String

Arrow

Bracer

Bow

Finger guard

Welsh origins

Bows have been used for thousands of years. Many of the early bows were made up of layers of horn, sinew and glue but the English longbow was made from one solid piece of wood. Many sorts of wood were used but yew was thought to be the best.

The English probably first realised the power of the longbow during the Welsh wars of the 12th century. By the late 13th century there were large numbers of archers in the English armies. They played a great part in many battles. Crecy in 1346, Poitiers in 1356 and Agincourt in 1415 were three of their greatest victories.

An ancient skill

The longbow needed strength, skill and plenty of practice. The pull was about 35-45 kg (80-100 lbs.), too strong to hold for very long. The skill came in being able to string the arrow, draw the bow, aim and release all in one swift, smooth movement. The string was held by the first three fingers of the right hand and the arrow rested on the top of the left hand. To protect his fingers the archer wore a leather guard. On his left arm he wore a bracer to stop the string slapping his arm.

To ensure that there were plenty of trained archers for the army men were obliged by law to practise archery. With practice, a good archer could get off up to 12 arrows in one minute. The longbow remained the main missile weapon until the 16th century.

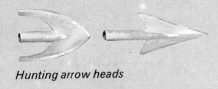

Hunting arrow heads

War arrow head

▲ Arrows were made by fletchers. They were about 770 mm (30 ins) long and usually made of birch. The shape of the point depended on its purpose. Hunting ones were broad and barbed. War arrows had long, narrow points.

▼ Goose, turkey and peacock feathers were used for arrows. They were bound and glued in place and set at a slight angle to make the arrow spin. At the tip was the nock, a groove to fit over the string.

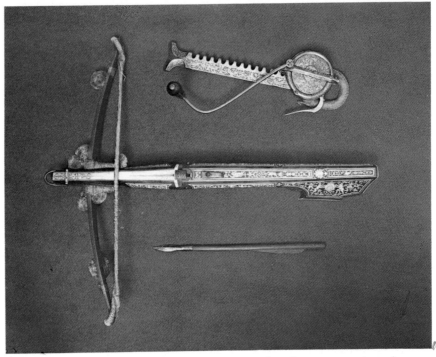

▲ The bolt or quarrel of this crossbow dates from the 16th century but the beautifully decorated crossbow is later. It was probably used for hunting and has a steel bow which means that it was very powerful. The steel cranequin was used to wind back the cord.

▼ Crossbows were extremely powerful and the bolts could easily penetrate plate armour. They were easy to load and aim but they had one great drawback: they were very slow. The bow was so powerful that the cord could not be pulled back by hand. The use of winders made it a very slow business.

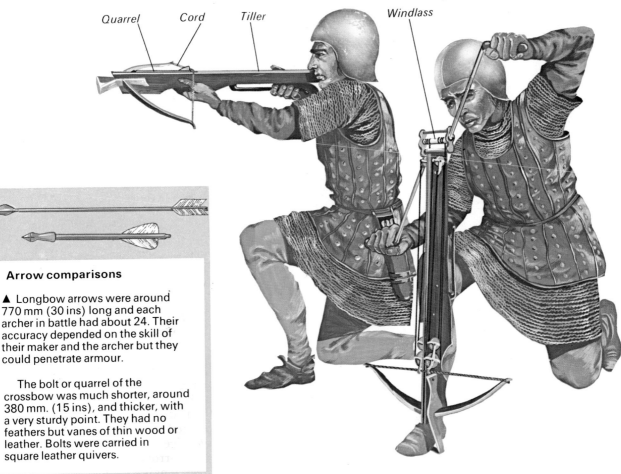

Quarrel *Cord* *Tiller* *Windlass*

Arrow comparisons

▲ Longbow arrows were around 770 mm (30 ins) long and each archer in battle had about 24. Their accuracy depended on the skill of their maker and the archer but they could penetrate armour.

The bolt or quarrel of the crossbow was much shorter, around 380 mm. (15 ins), and thicker, with a very sturdy point. They had no feathers but vanes of thin wood or leather. Bolts were carried in square leather quivers.

Full plate armour a skin of steel

▼ Whilst a knight might be fitted with a full harness, the ordinary foot soldier was less fortunate. His armour was likely to be old, odd pieces or a padded coat. Weapons were often farm tools on poles. If he was lucky he might capture a better weapon in battle.

The completely enclosed knight

The change over from mail to plate began about 1220 when metal plates were added at the knees. Once the idea was seen to be good the change over continued. By the middle of the 14th century legs, arms, head and parts of the body were protected by metal plates. Early in the 15th century the last plates were added and the entire body was covered by plate armour.

To allow easy movement of the body plates were often made in sections joined together by leather straps. This allowed the strips, or lames, to slide over each other without leaving any dangerous gaps for a sword to slip through.

Armours for war and peace

Armour was often known as a harness. It was known as a field armour if it was for use in war. Sometimes the field armour had extra plates which could be fitted on when the knight wanted to use it for tilt or tournament.

The feet were covered by narrow, overlapping plates making the sabatons. The lower part of the leg was enclosed in plate with special pieces at the knee. Only the front and outside of the thigh were protected by plate, although the inside might have some mail on it.

The breastplate of the armour was made thicker than the backplate. From the bottom of both hung a skirt of lames. The arms were covered in very much the same way as the legs and on the hands were gauntlets. These were leather gloves with metal plates fitted to them.

Styles of helmet

There were many shapes and styles of helmet since fashions changed. The great helm was so large that the base rested on the shoulders. The bascinet was lighter and had a moveable face piece called a visor. The armet and close helmet fitted around the head and both had visors, but they opened up differently.

The skill in making helmets or any pieces of armour lay in making it strong but not too heavy. The shape had to be just right so that a blow would be deflected and glance off. The full armour was made to be as comfortable as possible. It was not heavy enough to slow down the wearer very much.

The arming of a knight

▲ First to go on was a padded arming doublet which had patches of mail sewn on it. These protected places which were not very well covered by the plates.

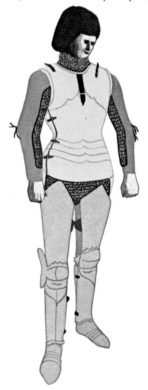

▲ Next to go on was the armour for the legs. These were strapped into place and held up by laces to the waist belt or by laces fastened on the doublet. Then the breast and back plates went on.

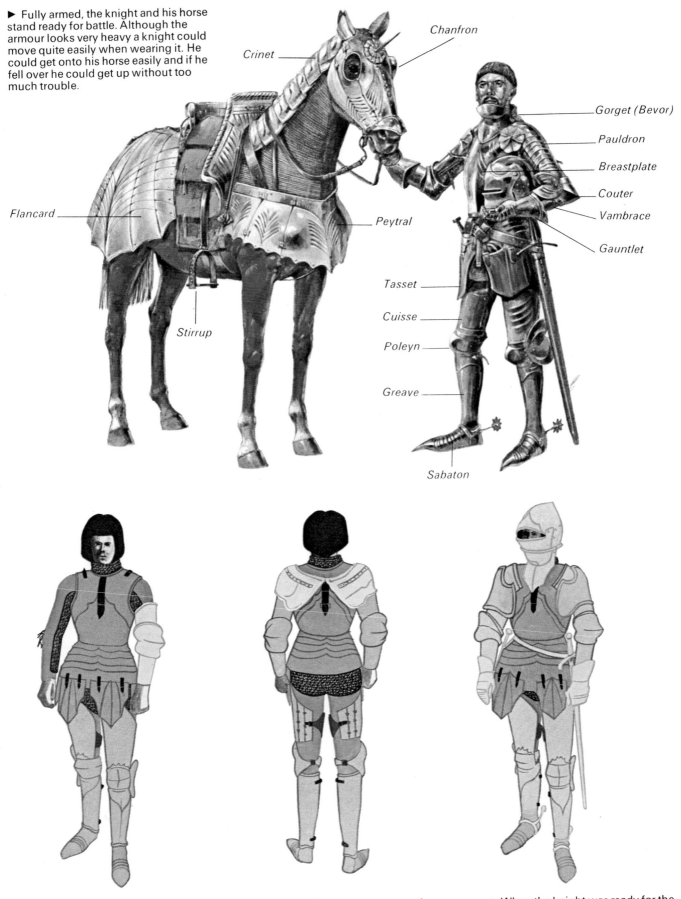

▶ Fully armed, the knight and his horse stand ready for battle. Although the armour looks very heavy a knight could move quite easily when wearing it. He could get onto his horse easily and if he fell over he could get up without too much trouble.

Crinet

Chanfron

Gorget (Bevor)

Pauldron

Breastplate

Couter

Vambrace

Gauntlet

Flancard

Peytral

Tasset

Cuisse

Poleyn

Greave

Stirrup

Sabaton

▲ Next came the arm pieces but not the gauntlets. The arm pieces, like those for the legs, were secured by laces and straps. All these parts of the armour had a padded lining.

▲ The last pieces to go on were the pauldrons or shoulder pieces. These were important pieces because the armpit was difficult to protect if the knight lifted his arm to strike a blow.

▲ When the knight was ready for the fight he put on his helmet and then his gauntlets. Helmets were left until last because they were stuffy and made the wearing of armour rather uncomfortable.

The great armourers

▶ **Maximilian Armour.** Named after the emperor of Austria, this style of armour was very popular with German and Austrian armourers. It was common from about 1500 to 1540. The surface was ridged to give extra strength and also to deflect blows. It had a close helmet which completely covered the head.

▼ **Gothic Armour.** This was one of the most graceful styles of armour and was made from about 1460 until 1500. It had some ridges and there were often brass edges to the plates. On the head is a helmet called a sallet.

Made to measure

During the 16th century the craft of armour-making reached its peak. Several towns in Italy and Germany became the main supply centres for the rest of Europe, though most countries made some armour and weapons. The armourers produced armours for war, for the tilt and elaborate ones for parades.

When armour was ordered the man's measurements were sent to the workshop who built up the armour piece by piece like a suit of clothes. Most workshops also produced quantities of cheaper armour for the ordinary soldier which were far less well-finished.

All the armours were carefully designed to give as much protection as possible. The shape and surfaces were planned to deflect a blow. Those pieces which covered the head and chest were thicker than the backplate where there was less danger of serious injury.

Italian and German armourers developed their own styles of armour which were fashionable at different times.

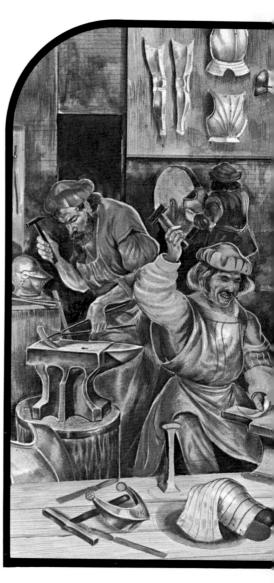

▶ Little is known about how armour was made but we do know that pieces were shaped by beating the cold metal over wooden or metal blocks called stakes. Many workshops had hammers driven by water wheels. When the armour was finished the pieces were often stamped with the mark of the armourer or the town.

◄ Black and White Armour. The metal was covered with a thick black paint and the borders polished bright. The paint protected the steel from rust. This light armour, called a three quarter suit, has an open faced helmet called a burgonet. Armour like this was used by light cavalry and many foot soldiers towards the end of the 16th century.

▼ Greenwich Armour. This armour was made at the royal workshop which Henry VIII set up at Greenwich just outside London. He brought over some foreign workers from Holland and Germany and they produced some very fine armours for the king and his friends. Many of the Greenwich armours, including some of the king's, have survived until today.

London

Solingen

Nurnberg

Paris

Passau

Augsburg

Innsbruck

Milan

Toledo

▲ This map shows the main armour and weapon-producing towns of Europe. Nuremberg, Augsburg and Milan produced most armour whilst swords came from Solingen, Passau and Toledo.

Armourers' marks

▼ In the big armour-producing towns there were guilds who stamped the armour with town marks. Many armourers added their personal marks as well.

Augsburg

Nuremberg

Solingen & Passau

The introduction of firearms

Gunpowder

10% sulphur

15% charcoal

75% saltpetre

Gunpowder is a mixture of sulphur, saltpetre and charcoal. The chemicals have been mixed in different proportions but usually the black powder is made up of 75% saltpetre, 15% charcoal and 10% sulphur. It is safe unless it is touched by a flame or a spark when it will immediately explode very violently indeed.

Guns and gunpowder

It is not known for certain when gunpowder was first used but the Chinese had some very crude bamboo guns by the 12th century. Some time later, knowledge of the powder reached Europe. The first known mention of European guns is in a manuscript written in 1326.

At first gunpowder was used only for cannons but before long some small handguns were developed. These were simply hollow tubes with a small hole drilled through the side at one end which was blocked. The barrel was fixed to a length of wood or metal.

Powder was poured down the barrel and followed by a bullet of stone or lead. These were rammed down hard and the weapon was ready to fire. A pinch of powder was placed over the small hole. A piece of glowing ember or a hot iron was touched to the powder which then exploded and blew the bullet out of the barrel.

Later the glowing ember was replaced by a piece of cord called a match. It was soaked in a solution of saltpetre and allowed to dry. The match burned very slowly so it could be carried in the hand and used to fire the handgun.

Musketeers and pikemen

A later development was the serpentine, a metal arm fitted at the side of the wooden stock to hold the match. One end of the serpentine was pressed and the other end holding the match swung down to touch the match to the powder. Later the serpentine was made to work by means of a trigger and springs.

The gun's wooden body was shaped to make it easier to hold and shoot and the gun became known as a matchlock musket. Towards the end of the 16th century most armies had large numbers of troops using these muskets.

Musket drill

The musketeers learned a drill for loading and firing their muskets. While they were reloading their weapons were useless and if they were attacked they could do little to defend themselves. To protect them during this time groups of pikemen were spaced among the musketeers. They were armed with pikes about 5m (16.4 ft) long with which they could hold off most attacks.

The main drawback of the matchlock was that the match had to be kept alight and it could be put out of action by the wind or rain.

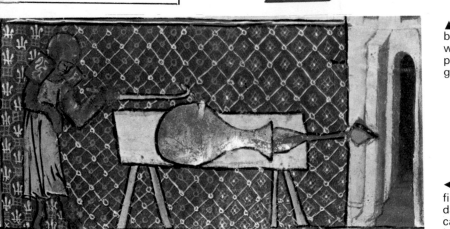

▲ Early handguns were very simple with a barrel fastened to a wooden stock. They were fired by means of a lever holding a piece of burning cord which pressed the glowing end into a pan holding some powder.

◄ The first known picture of a European firearm is in the margin of a manuscript dating from 1326. It shows a vase-shaped cannon being fired by a knight in armour. It is fixed on a bench and fires an arrow.

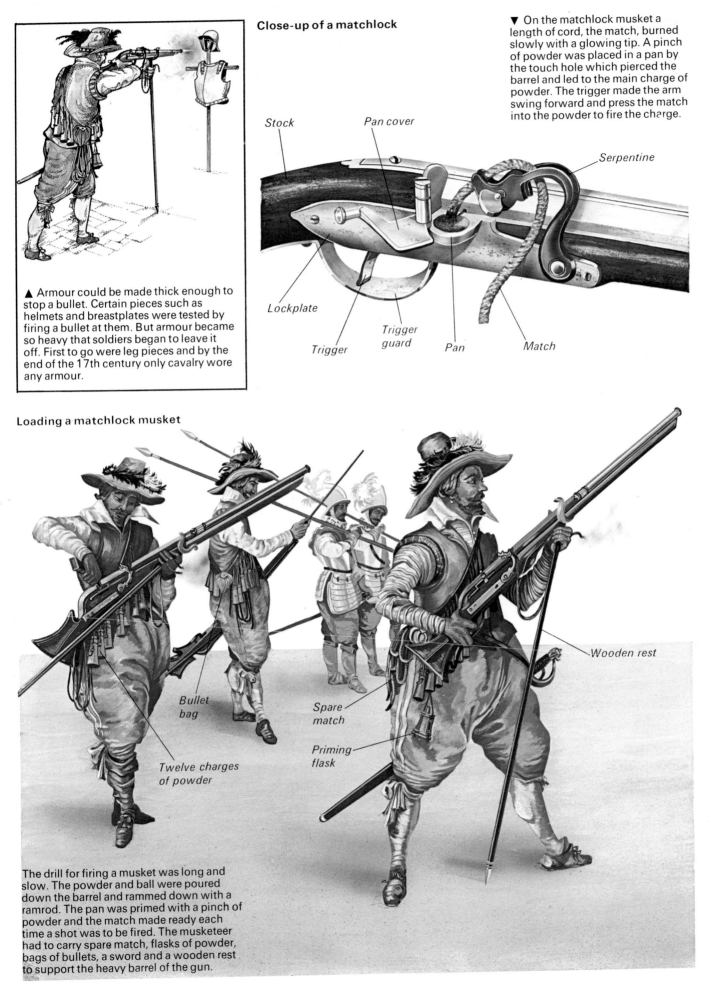

Close-up of a matchlock

▼ On the matchlock musket a length of cord, the match, burned slowly with a glowing tip. A pinch of powder was placed in a pan by the touch hole which pierced the barrel and led to the main charge of powder. The trigger made the arm swing forward and press the match into the powder to fire the charge.

Stock

Pan cover

Serpentine

Lockplate

Trigger

Trigger guard

Pan

Match

▲ Armour could be made thick enough to stop a bullet. Certain pieces such as helmets and breastplates were tested by firing a bullet at them. But armour became so heavy that soldiers began to leave it off. First to go were leg pieces and by the end of the 17th century only cavalry wore any armour.

Loading a matchlock musket

Bullet bag

Twelve charges of powder

Spare match

Priming flask

Wooden rest

The drill for firing a musket was long and slow. The powder and ball were poured down the barrel and rammed down with a ramrod. The pan was primed with a pinch of powder and the match made ready each time a shot was to be fired. The musketeer had to carry spare match, flasks of powder, bags of bullets, a sword and a wooden rest to support the heavy barrel of the gun.

War games

Warlike practices
Like all jobs war needs practice and
knights spent some of their time playing
at war. One simple method was the
quintain, which was made with a
pivoted arm at the top of a pole. At one
end of the arm was a target and at the
other a weight. When the target was hit
by a lance, the weight swung round and
hit an unwary rider a hefty clout.

A more dangerous war game was the
melée, which was fought in a field or
open space and was a form of miniature
battle. Sometimes the practice battle
became the real thing and people were
killed and wounded.

As time went on the tournament became organized with sets of rules.
Special armour and blunted weapons
were sometimes used.

Single combat
Many knights felt that the tournament
with so many taking part did not give
them a chance to show their skill at
arms. They preferred single combat,
which was known as jousting. In a
friendly contest the jousters used blunted weapons but if there was a quarrel
they used normal weapons. Sometimes
the fight continued until one was dead.

The knights might use sword, club,
lance or dagger. About 1420 a new form
of joust was introduced. A long fence
separated the two riders and reduced
the chance of the horses colliding.

This new style of joust was called
tilting and there were many kinds of
competition with different rules. Points
were scored by striking the opponent on
the helmet or on the body. Valuable
prizes were often awarded to the winner.

Armour for the tilt
Tilting armour was specially made and
was usually much stronger and heavier
than armour for war. Sometimes extra-
strong pieces were fitted onto an ordinary war armour. Often the legs had no
armour but were protected by steel
plates fitted to the front of the saddle.
Most tilting was done on horseback but
some contests were fought on foot, also
in specially made armours.

Tilting and tournaments gradually
became less popular and by the end of
the 17th century they had almost died
out.

A melée

▲ This German armour was designed for a form of jousting in which the aim was to break the lance by hitting the opponent square and hard. The helmet was bolted to the breastplate. A long bar was fitted to one side to support the lance.

◄ This scene shows a melée, or miniature battle, at a tournament. Dozens of knights fight one another just as in war except that nobody should be killed. If a knight fell his helper, a squire, was expected to save him from harm by dragging him out of the mob. Special stands were set up for spectators. The tournament consisted of many different events and might go on for a week.

India fashions in the East

Indian weapons

▲ Indian weapon makers liked to produce beautiful pieces. This is a steel axe made in the shape of a deer's head. The eyes are small rubies and the whole weapon has some decoration.

▲ This is a three way knife. It is held by the bar in the centre and can be used to stab forward with the short blade or to slash in either direction with the other two.

▲ This was a secret weapon called the "tiger claws". The fingers were slipped through the holes and the blades covered by the closed fist. When ready the holder opened his hand and slashed.

▼ The *pata* was a sword blade fitted with a metal gauntlet. Inside this was a metal bar which was gripped by the warrior. He held the *pata* forward like a lance but he could also slash with it like a sword.

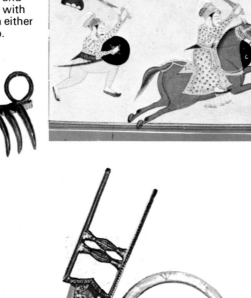

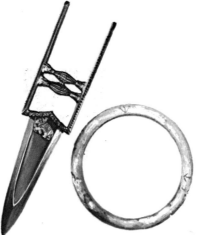

▲ This 18th century Indian miniature shows an elephant being attacked by horsemen armed with spears and swords. Elephants were often used in war by the Indians and some even wore specially-made armour. On their backs they carried archers or men armed with matchlocks.

◀ This is called a *katar* or punch dagger. The two bars in the middle were held in the clenched fist so that the blade stuck forward. To stab, the Indian gave a jab forward just like a punch in boxing.

◀ The flat steel hoop with a sharpened edge was called a *chakram*. The warrior sent it spinning through the air just like a quoit. It was a deadly weapon used by the fierce Sikhs.

Armour in the East

As firearms became more efficient, the wearing of armour gradually died out in Europe. But further east it was still worn for several hundred years.

Indian armour was not the same as the European form. The helmets very seldom had pieces to cover the face although most had a kind of mail coif. On the body most warriors wore mail with metal plates attached. Some had clothing which was padded and strengthened with small plates. Round shields were popular. Most of the armour, helmets and shields were finely decorated with carving and inset with precious metals.

India is a vast country which produced many different kinds of weapons. The firearms were copies of those made in Europe and the matchlock was used in India for centuries after it was out of date in Europe.

A great variety of cutting weapons were used. The most usual sword was called a *talwar* and it had a single edged, slightly curved blade. The hilt was fairly plain with a single knuckle guard. Other swords had great blades which curved at weird angles. A few swords had hilts big enough to allow a two-handed grip.

Beautiful weapons

Daggers were common throughout India. Some were as big as small swords and others had blades which curved in all directions. One of the best known was the *kukri* which was used by the Ghurkas from Nepal. Many of the Indian daggers had very beautiful hilts which were decorated with precious metals, jade or jewels.

Indian armourers made a speciality of combined weapons and many of the axes and maces had thin daggers hidden in their handles.

The Indians used bows made from steel and some composite bows decorated with paintings. They used many different types of arrow including some like those of the British longbow.

Persia, Turkey and other nearby countries used arms and armour which were very similar to those of India. Persian helmets were usually slightly bigger whilst Turkish armour was more of a mixture of mail and plate. The Persians used a very curved type of sword known as a *shamshir*.

Plumes

Kulah kud (helmet)

Mail

Armour

Khandar (sword)

Matchlock

▲ An Indian warrior in 18th century armour. On his head he has a helmet fitted with a fringe of mail. His face is protected by a sliding nasal bar. His armour is a mixture of padding, mail and steel plates. He carries a long, double edged sword and a matchlock.

Japan

Japanese archery

Japanese warriors made great use of archery and were experts at using the bow on horseback. They had miniature bows and arrows which they carried on coaches to protect themselves on journeys. Their bows were usually decorated.

Arrow heads

▲ Japanese metal work was always of the best quality. Even the arrow heads were finely polished and pierced. Each shape was for a special purpose. The one on the right was a rope cutter.

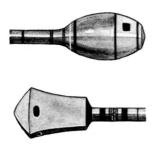

Whistling arrows

▲ One way to frighten an enemy is to make a lot of noise. The Japanese used arrows with specially designed hollow heads. As they flew through the air they made a loud whistling.

▶ This Japanese screen painting shows a Samurai general at the Battle of the Uji River in 1184. His armour is made up of many small lacquered pieces laced into sections with white silk. The helmet has a wide protective backpiece and curved sides. As a general, he is entitled to wear a gilded horned crest on his helmet.

Samurai

Japanese craftsmen were among the best in the world and their swords and armour were of the finest quality. Their armour was quite different from that of Europe. The helmets were given very wide sweeping sidepieces and often had fierce looking facepieces. The armour itself was made of many small plates which were laced together into large sections. Some larger plates and pieces of mail were also used.

The warriors of Japan were known as Samurai and much of the history of the country is taken up with battles between various groups of the Samurai families. Like the European knight the Samurai had to have some way of being recognised. Some wore large crests on their helmets whilst others had small flags fastened to the back of their armour.

Japanese bows were rather unusual. They were about 2 m. (6.6 ft) long and were held, not in the middle, but about a third of the way up. This made them easier to use on horseback. The bow and arrows were often carried in one case. Japanese archers used a great variety of arrows with many different types of head, each one designed for a different job. Many Japanese foot soldiers also carried polearms.

The perfect sword

In order to cut really well a sword needs a very hard edge, but if it is too hard the metal will shatter. To stop it shattering the metal must be soft.

Swordsmiths all over the world had to balance these opposites and the Japanese came closest to finding a perfect balance. They produced a blade which was very hard outside and softer inside. The blade was slightly curved and very brightly polished. The hilt was very simple without the bars and guards found on most European swords.

The grip was wrapped round with black lacing and the guard, the *tsuba*, was a flat plate, often beautifully decorated. The scabbards were quite plain and made of black lacquered wood.

Sword types

A Samurai warrior carried two swords pushed through the sash at his waist: a long one called the *katana*, and a short one called the *wakizashi*.

The *wakizashi* was kept in a sheath with two slits at the sides. These held a small knife and a tool which the Samurai used when he combed his hair. For festivals and ceremonies the Samurai had an extra long sword called a *tachi*, which was very decorative.

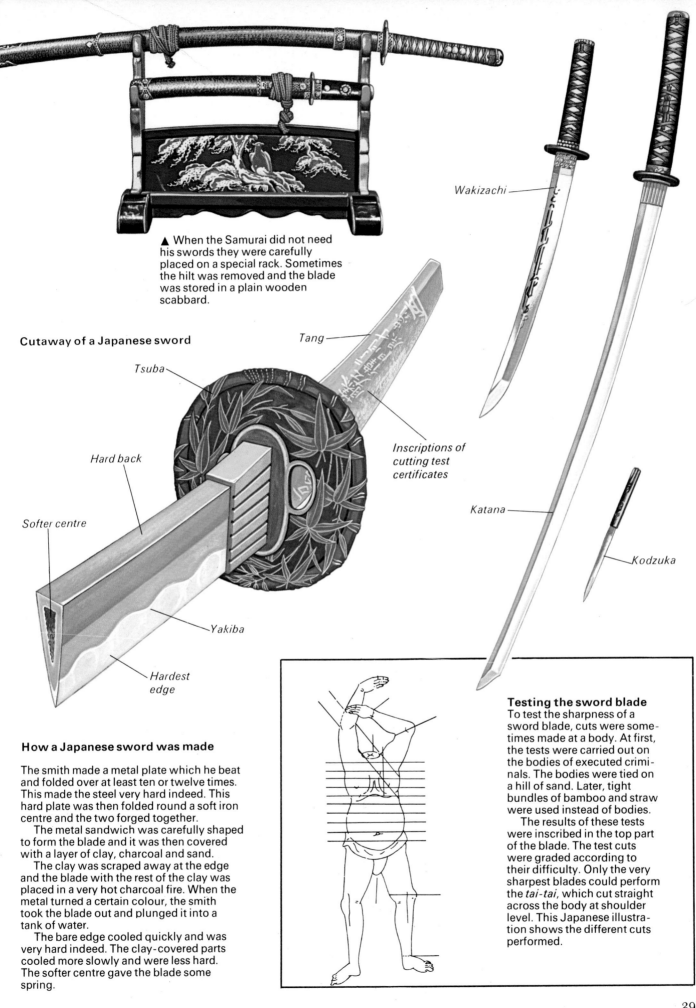

▲ When the Samurai did not need his swords they were carefully placed on a special rack. Sometimes the hilt was removed and the blade was stored in a plain wooden scabbard.

Wakizachi

Cutaway of a Japanese sword

Tang

Tsuba

Hard back

Inscriptions of cutting test certificates

Softer centre

Katana

Kodzuka

Yakiba

Hardest edge

How a Japanese sword was made

The smith made a metal plate which he beat and folded over at least ten or twelve times. This made the steel very hard indeed. This hard plate was then folded round a soft iron centre and the two forged together.

The metal sandwich was carefully shaped to form the blade and it was then covered with a layer of clay, charcoal and sand.

The clay was scraped away at the edge and the blade with the rest of the clay was placed in a very hot charcoal fire. When the metal turned a certain colour, the smith took the blade out and plunged it into a tank of water.

The bare edge cooled quickly and was very hard indeed. The clay-covered parts cooled more slowly and were less hard. The softer centre gave the blade some spring.

Testing the sword blade

To test the sharpness of a sword blade, cuts were some-times made at a body. At first, the tests were carried out on the bodies of executed crimi-nals. The bodies were tied on a hill of sand. Later, tight bundles of bamboo and straw were used instead of bodies.

The results of these tests were inscribed in the top part of the blade. The test cuts were graded according to their difficulty. Only the very sharpest blades could perform the *tai-tai*, which cut straight across the body at shoulder level. This Japanese illustra-tion shows the different cuts performed.

29

Changing styles of swordplay

◀ The *landsknechts* were German mercenaries who fought for anyone. One of their weapons was the two-handed sword. These were whirled around the head but could also be used as a kind of short lance. The *landsknecht* also carried a short sword and a dagger.

▼ In the 17th century, fighting with weapons such as the left-handed dagger and rapier was very popular. The dagger was used for both attack and defence. A cloak sometimes took the place of the dagger and was wrapped around the forearm as a simple means of defence.

Slashing swords

When men made the first copper and bronze swords they were often cutting weapons. The blade was long and broad and the sword was used to slash with. Most of the early swords were used in this way and there was little skill in individual combat. The combatants just slashed at one another and blocked the blows with their shields.

The Roman soldier was an exception to this rule as he was encouraged to use the point of his sword. But for over 1,000 years after the Romans, the sword remained principally a slashing weapon.

As armour became stronger and better designed, sword cuts had less and less effect. The point became more important and special thrusting swords were made. These were called estocs and had thick, stiff blades with a sharp point which was intended to penetrate the weak parts of an armour. They were held in both hands.

Cut and thrust

During the Middle Ages more and more use was made of the point and in the 16th century the swordsmith produced the rapier, a sword designed mainly for thrusting.

Rapiers were usually long with a stiff, thrusting blade. The hilt had a series of bars to protect the hand. In the early 17th century the bars were replaced by a deep metal bowl: this was the cup-hilted rapier. It was very popular in Spain where it was used long after the rest of Europe had given it up. The Spaniards also used a rapier and a left-handed dagger together.

The end of an era

During the 17th century the rapier became less popular and its place was taken by the small sword. This was light with a straight blade and a simple hilt which was often finely decorated. By the end of the 18th century the fashion of wearing swords had died out and the small sword was only worn by a few officials.

There was much argument about the best kind of military sword. Some claimed that one for stabbing was best, others wanted one for slashing. The argument was never settled as firearms made swords unnecessary.

◄ In the 18th century most gentlemen learned to use the sword. The style of fighting was called fencing and there were many schools at which it was taught. Most teachers had their own special style. Fencing is still taught today.

▼ This dashing painting by Théodore Géricault shows the colour and finery of the 18th and 19th century uniforms. Many of the cavalry used a slashing curved sword like the one carried by this officer of the French Imperial Guard. This type of sword was known as a sabre.

Daggers
Daggers were among the first edged weapons used and they rather died out after the 17th century. They were replaced by bayonets which served as weapons or tools.

◄ Rondel Dagger
This form of dagger was used by knights in the 14th century. It had a long, stiff blade and the hilt was made with two discs, one at the top and one at the bottom of the grip. They were carried on the right of the waist.

◄ Stiletto
These were popular in Italy in the 16th and 17th centuries. The blade was fairly short, thin and square. The hilt was often of steel like the blade. Some stilettos had the blade marked as a kind of ruler to help the gunner.

◄ Scottish Dirk
These were often made from cut down pieces of sword blades. The hilt was short and cut from wood, with a flat, rounded end. In the 19th century they were made with fancy sheaths holding a small knife and fork.

Wheellock and flintlock mechanical methods

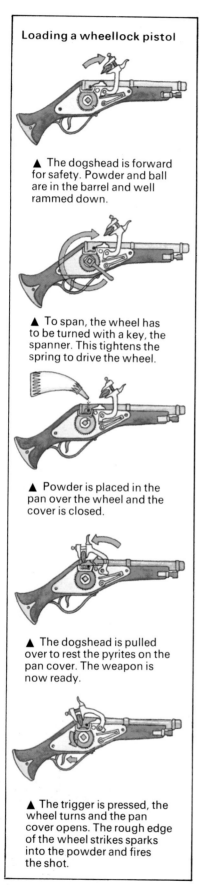

Loading a wheellock pistol

▲ The dogshead is forward for safety. Powder and ball are in the barrel and well rammed down.

▲ To span, the wheel has to be turned with a key, the spanner. This tightens the spring to drive the wheel.

▲ Powder is placed in the pan over the wheel and the cover is closed.

▲ The dogshead is pulled over to rest the pyrites on the pan cover. The weapon is now ready.

▲ The trigger is pressed, the wheel turns and the pan cover opens. The rough edge of the wheel strikes sparks into the powder and fires the shot.

Flying sparks

The matchlock was a cheap and simple weapon but it had drawbacks. Gunmakers looked for ways to improve firearms and early in the 16th century the wheellock was invented.

The wheellock had a steel wheel driven round by a spring. The edge was rough and pressed against a piece of mineral called pyrites. As the wheel turned it made a shower of sparks which fell into some powder near the touch hole and fired the shot. Before each shot the spring was wound up by turning the wheel with a special metal key called a spanner.

The piece of pyrites was held between two jaws at the end of a metal arm called the dogshead. If the dogshead was pushed back the pyrites was clear of the wheel and there was no danger of the weapon being fired accidentally.

The mechanism of the wheellock was complicated but it was possible to make locks small enough to fit onto a small firearm and so for the first time it was possible to make a pistol. Wheellocks were expensive but many rich people ordered them and had them beautifully decorated with inlaid metal or horn. The long wheellock guns had only a short butt which was held to the cheek when being fired.

A more reliable lock

The wheellock was very good but it was complicated and therefore expensive. It was also inclined to jam. Gunmakers looked for simpler, cheaper methods of firing the powder.

A French gunmaker found the answer early in the 17th century. He made a lock which used flint and steel to produce sparks. An arm with two jaws held a flat piece of flint. The pan was covered by an L-shaped piece of steel. When the trigger was pressed the arm swung forward and the flint scraped down the flat steel face and made sparks. At the same time the arm and flint pushed the L-shaped pan cover clear of the pan, so the sparks fell into the pan and fired the powder.

The flintlock was reliable and cheap to make. It could be made in any size and was fitted to every kind of firearm, large and small. It was used for over 200 years and was not replaced until the middle of the 19th century. Some flintlock guns could fire more than one shot but most were single shot weapons.

▼ This is part of a fine 17th century wheellock rifle. It was made for a rich man who would have used it for hunting. These weapons were beautifully decorated with gold, ivory, horn and steel.

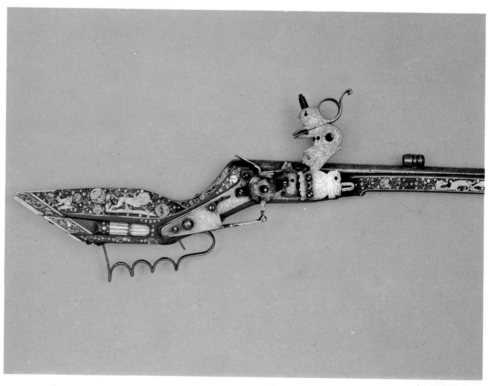

An 18th century blunderbuss

Spring bayonet

Butt

Lock

Ramrod

Muzzle

◀ The blunderbuss had a barrel with a very wide muzzle. It was thought that this would spread the shot but it made little difference. The gun was loaded with several small balls.

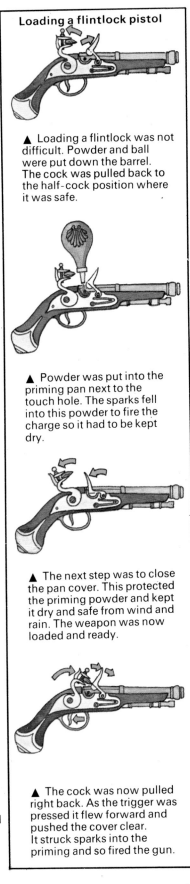

Loading a flintlock pistol

▲ Loading a flintlock was not difficult. Powder and ball were put down the barrel. The cock was pulled back to the half-cock position where it was safe.

▲ Powder was put into the priming pan next to the touch hole. The sparks fell into this powder to fire the charge so it had to be kept dry.

▲ The next step was to close the pan cover. This protected the priming powder and kept it dry and safe from wind and rain. The weapon was now loaded and ready.

▲ The cock was now pulled right back. As the trigger was pressed it flew forward and pushed the cover clear. It struck sparks into the priming and so fired the gun.

▲ Travelling was very dangerous and many coaches were stopped and robbed by highwaymen. Many coaches carried a guard and it was usual for him to carry a blunderbuss to protect the coach. The mail coach guard carried two flintlock pistols as well as the blunderbuss.

The search for accuracy

Rifles versus smoothbore

The British troops in the 18th century were armed with muskets. The barrel was simply a metal tube which meant that the musket, nicknamed Brown Bess, was not very accurate.

When fighting broke out between the British and the American colonists in 1776, the British soon found that some of the colonists were excellent shots. One of the main reasons was that they were using rifles, which are far more accurate weapons. The colonist's rifle had a very long barrel and fired a bullet much smaller than that of the Brown Bess.

The origin of the rifle

The American rifle was known as the Kentucky or Pennsylvania long rifle although it was not only made in these states. Its barrel was about 1.1 m. (45 ins) long and the bullet was about 13 mm. (0.5 in) in diameter.

The rifle stock was usually made of walnut wood. There was plenty of decoration and in the butt was a cavity fitted with a fancy brass lid. This box held patches which were wrapped around lead bullets before they were loaded.

The butt of the Pennsylvanian rifle drooped and had a very deep cutout where it fitted against the shoulder. The rifle developed from hunting rifles which were taken to America by German settlers.

Despite the fact that they could see how good and accurate the rifle was the British Army did not start to use rifles until just after 1800 during the Napoleonic Wars.

▼ British troops wore bright red coats which made them easy to spot. They were often ambushed by the Americans who were experts in this kind of surprise warfare.

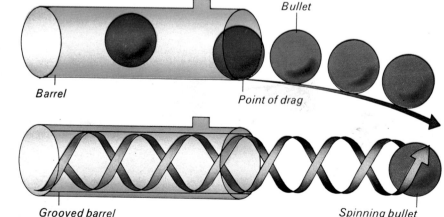

Why the rifle was more accurate

Bullet

Barrel

Point of drag

Grooved barrel

Spinning bullet

◄ A bullet travelling along a smooth barrel bounced along the inside. As it left the muzzle it might drag on one spot which meant that the bullet was thrown very slightly to one side. The next one might drag at a different point. No two were ever exactly the same.

◄ In a rifle barrel there were a number of shallow grooves cut on the inside. As the tight fitting bullet went down the barrel these spiral grooves turned the bullet and made it spin. This helped to correct any swinging off course and it flew straight and true.

▼ The long rifle was usually loaded from a powder flask. Some powder went into the pan and a charge down the barrel. The round bullet was wrapped in a greased patch of linen or thin leather and pushed down with the ramrod. It had to fit very tightly.

◄ Many of the American troops wore uniforms but many also wore their ordinary clothes. They fought very hard and had learnt the art of sudden, surprise attacks.

◄ Bullets were simply lead balls. The lead was melted in a crucible, scooped out and poured into a metal mould. It filled the mould, cooled and set hard. The mould opened down the middle and out fell the bullet.

▼ This man is making cartridges for a rifle or musket. They were kept in a special pouch.

Mould

Metal scoop

Crucible

Former *Bullet*

Cartridge paper

Patch and bullet

▲ To make a cartridge, paper was cut to size and shape and rolled round a wooden former. One end was twisted together and a measure of powder poured in. Next the bullet was pressed down the tube on top of the powder and other end was tightly twisted together.

18th century breech-loading rifle

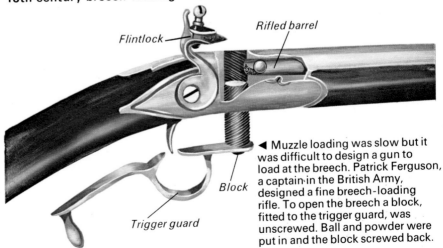

Flintlock

Rifled barrel

Block

Trigger guard

◄ Muzzle loading was slow but it was difficult to design a gun to load at the breech. Patrick Ferguson, a captain in the British Army, designed a fine breech-loading rifle. To open the breech a block, fitted to the trigger guard, was unscrewed. Ball and powder were put in and the block screwed back.

35

The percussion system a chemical change

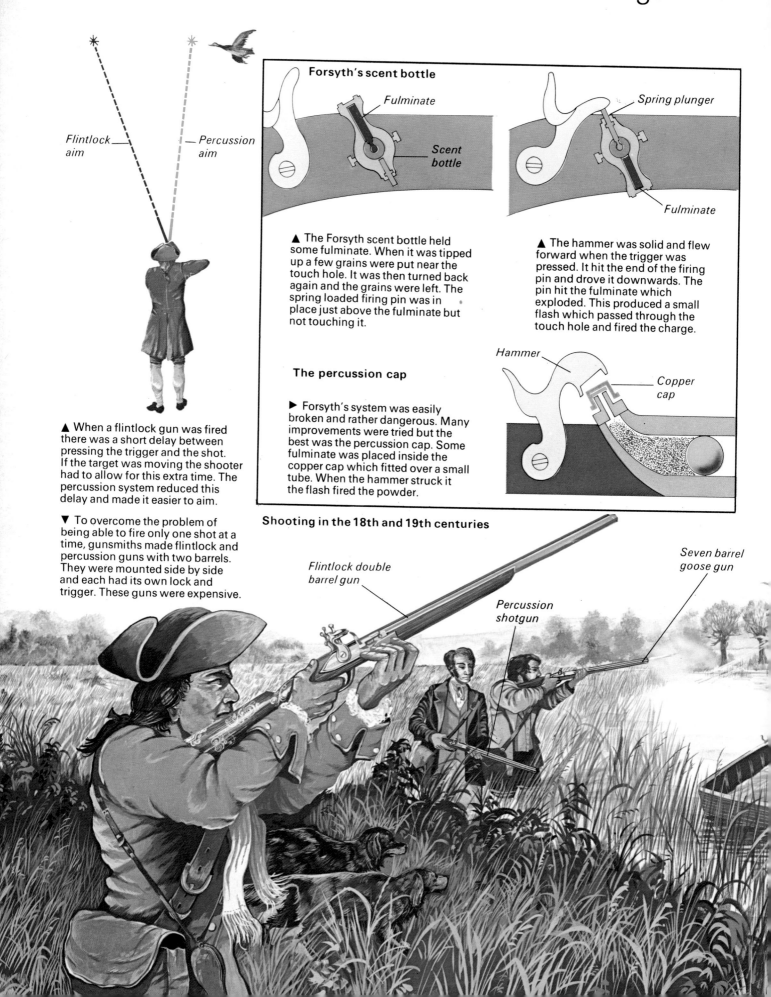

Flintlock aim — Percussion aim

▲ When a flintlock gun was fired there was a short delay between pressing the trigger and the shot. If the target was moving the shooter had to allow for this extra time. The percussion system reduced this delay and made it easier to aim.

▼ To overcome the problem of being able to fire only one shot at a time, gunsmiths made flintlock and percussion guns with two barrels. They were mounted side by side and each had its own lock and trigger. These guns were expensive.

Forsyth's scent bottle

Fulminate
Scent bottle
Spring plunger
Fulminate

▲ The Forsyth scent bottle held some fulminate. When it was tipped up a few grains were put near the touch hole. It was then turned back again and the grains were left. The spring loaded firing pin was in place just above the fulminate but not touching it.

The percussion cap

▶ Forsyth's system was easily broken and rather dangerous. Many improvements were tried but the best was the percussion cap. Some fulminate was placed inside the copper cap which fitted over a small tube. When the hammer struck it the flash fired the powder.

▲ The hammer was solid and flew forward when the trigger was pressed. It hit the end of the firing pin and drove it downwards. The pin hit the fulminate which exploded. This produced a small flash which passed through the touch hole and fired the charge.

Hammer
Copper cap

Shooting in the 18th and 19th centuries

Flintlock double barrel gun
Percussion shotgun
Seven barrel goose gun

Drawbacks of the flintlock

The flintlock worked extremely well for over 200 years but it had its drawbacks. The priming powder could be ruined by wind or rain. The flint wore out and had to be changed after about 30 shots. Also, the gun did not work every time.

There was also the delay known as the hangfire. When the trigger was pressed it took some time for the cock to fly forward, for the flint to strike sparks and for these to fall into the pan. The priming powder then had to flare and the flash had to pass through the touch hole to ignite the main charge and cause the explosion.

When the target was a moving one, such as a flying bird, the gun had to be pointed ahead of it to allow for movement during this hangfire time. Hunters also found that the flash of the priming powder often scared the target and it started to move before the bullet had left the barrel.

A chemical solution

One of the hunters who found all these problems very annoying was a Scottish clergyman named Alexander Forsyth. He was a hunter but he was also a keen chemist and he had heard about some special chemicals called fulminates. These chemicals are very unstable which means that they will explode if they just get a hard knock.

Forsyth's "scent bottle"

Forsyth tried some experiments in which he used fulminates instead of gunpowder to load his guns. He found they did not work very well but it gave him the idea of using them in place of priming powder. He tried many methods and finally produced his "scent bottle".

Early in the 19th century Forsyth patented his idea and people soon realized how much better the system could be. Other inventors took up his idea and tried to improve on it.

Finally, someone came up with the idea of a copper percussion cap. The fulminate was on the inside at the top of the cap. This was pushed over a small metal pillar through which a little hole led through the barrel to the main charge of powder.

A metal hammer took the place of the old cock and pressure on the trigger made this bang down on to the cap. This caused the fulminate to explode and the flash passed through the hole to the powder and fired the shot.

The cap was easy to load on to the pillar, it seldom failed to fire and the hangfire was much less. The whole system was a big improvement on the old flintlock. Soon gunsmiths were making percussion guns of all kinds and all sizes, and they also converted the old flintlock guns to the new system.

A shot tower

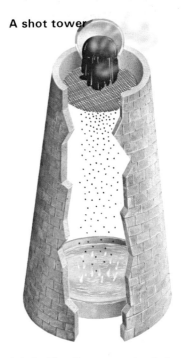

▲ In battle a firearm was loaded with a single bullet but for sport the load was a large number of small lead balls. This was called shot and was made by pouring molten lead through a sieve at the top of a tall tower. As the lead fell through the air it became round. It fell into water at the bottom and cooled.

Punt gun

Breech-loading shotguns

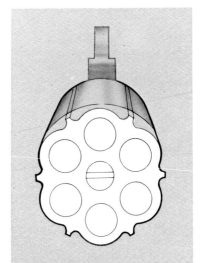

▲ Close-up of the barrels of a pepperbox pistol. On this weapon each of the six barrels was fired separately. The barrels were drilled into a solid block of metal and the weapon was rather clumsy. Pepperboxes were an early form of revolver.

Metal cartridges and rapid fire

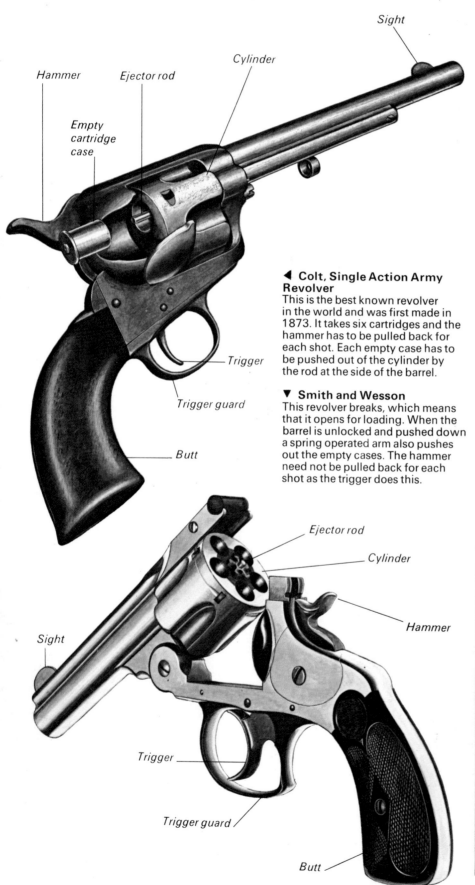

Sight

Cylinder

Hammer

Ejector rod

Empty
cartridge
case

Trigger

Trigger guard

Butt

◀ **Colt, Single Action Army Revolver**
This is the best known revolver in the world and was first made in 1873. It takes six cartridges and the hammer has to be pulled back for each shot. Each empty case has to be pushed out of the cylinder by the rod at the side of the barrel.

▼ **Smith and Wesson**
This revolver breaks, which means that it opens for loading. When the barrel is unlocked and pushed down a spring operated arm also pushes out the empty cases. The hammer need not be pulled back for each shot as the trigger does this.

Ejector rod

Cylinder

Hammer

Sight

Trigger

Trigger guard

Butt

A century of changes

Most flintlock and percussion guns were single shot weapons. Some flintlock revolvers were made but they were not reliable. In 1836 Samuel Colt patented a percussion revolver which was very good. He made many others and all worked well but they were still difficult to load. What was wanted was a way of loading at the breech.

In 1857 Smith and Wesson produced a revolver which did this and also used a metal cartridge. The metal cartridge was soon improved and by the 1870s the centre-fire cartridge was in general use. Metal cartridges were soon used in many kinds of automatic repeaters as it was so much easier to load them.

Machine guns such as the Gatling gun were worked by hand, but by the end of the century guns which fired themselves were common. Machine guns like the Maxim would go on firing for as long as ammunition was fed into them.

Foggy battles

Another change was the use of smokeless powder. Black powder gave off a great deal of smoke, so battles in the past had been fought in a kind of mist.

There were also changes in the design of bullets. In place of the round ball most guns now fired a pointed, streamlined bullet, often covered with a thin coat of nickel or copper. Their range and power were greatly increased.

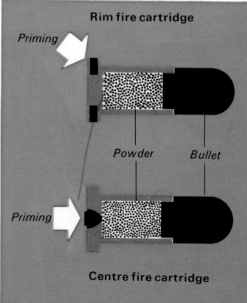

Rim fire cartridge

Priming

Powder   Bullet

Priming

Centre fire cartridge

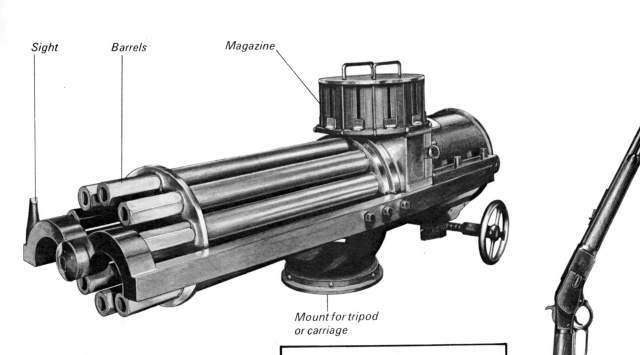

Sight Barrels Magazine

Mount for tripod
or carriage

▲ The Gatling Gun
An American doctor invented this hand
worked machine gun in 1861. It had six
barrels spaced around a central shaft and
when the handle was turned the barrels
rotated. The ammunition was held in a
magazine on top of the barrels.

On the first Gatling guns the cartridges
were of paper and had a percussion cap to
fire them but later metal cased cartridges
were used. The gun worked very well and
was part of the equipment of many armies.
The later ones could fire 3,000 shots a
minute. Some were mounted on wheeled
carriages and saw action in battles in many
parts of the world.

One of the very latest high speed American
guns, the Vulcan, uses the same idea and
fires over 6,000 rounds a minute.

How the Gatling Gun worked
The cartridge dropped into the
breech of a barrel and a series of
levers pushed it home. When it
reached the bottom position a
striker fired it. As the barrel turned
the empty case was ejected. This
happened with each barrel.

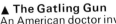

▲ Winchester Repeating Rifle
The cartridges are loaded into a
tube beneath the barrel. When the
trigger guard lever is pulled down a
cartridge is pulled out of the tube.
As it is closed the cartridge is
placed in the breech to be fired.
When the lever is pressed again
the empty case is thrown out and a
new one loaded.

◄ Rim Fire Cartridges
The first metal case cartridge had
the fulminate inside a small raised
rim at its base. This was hit by the
hammer and fired the charge. This
kind of cartridge is still used for
small calibre guns. Calibre refers to
the diameter of the bullet.

◄ Centre Fire Cartridges
The fulminate is in a small cap,
the primer, set in the middle of the
cartridge base. This is the type used
in almost every modern weapon.
The primer is struck by a metal pin
set in the front of the hammer. It is
also used in shotgun cartridges
used for hunting.

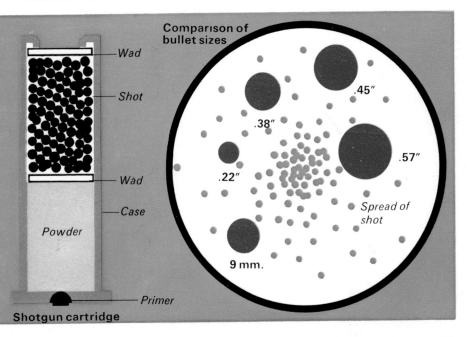

Wad

Shot

Wad

Case

Powder

Primer

Shotgun cartridge

Comparison of
bullet sizes

.45"

.38"

.57"

.22"

Spread of
shot

9 mm.

World War I

▼ Aircraft played an important part in World War I, the first war in which they were involved. They were used as spotters for artillery, as bombers and for attacking enemy troops. Airships were also used for bombing raids.

▼ At first, trenches were quite simple, but as the war went on they became very complex. Off the trenches were deep dug-outs in which the men lived and some were used as command posts. The dug-outs and trenches were all linked together by field telephones. Life in the trenches was very unpleasant, especially in wet weather.

A different kind of war

In 1914 fighting started between Germany and her allies and Britain and hers. The war was expected to be over quickly, but it lasted over four years. It became a trench war with both sides settled in long lines of dugouts joined by trenches and protected with barbed wire.

Both sides tried every way to break through these strong defences. Artillery sent down showers of high explosive shells and the troops tried to rush across the open ground known as "no man's land", and capture the trenches. Most attacks were beaten back and casualties were enormous.

The machine gun played a very important part in the war and made cavalry completely out of date. Troops on both sides were armed with repeating rifles and the officers had revolvers or automatic pistols.

Tanks and gas

World War I was the first war in which aircraft played a major part. They were used as bombers, as fighters and for observation. Motor cars and cycles were also used, but the most important invention was the tank. It was fitted with armoured plates to keep out the bullets and caterpillar tracks to help it cross rough and uneven ground.

Another new idea developed was the use of poison gas. It was fired in shells or released from cylinders to blow across the battlefield. All the troops had to carry respirators or gas-masks.

The return of armour

The men were in trenches below ground level so there were many head wounds. By about 1915 most of the troops wore some kind of steel helmet. Some machine gunners were even fitted with thick body armour.

German attack on a British trench, 1917

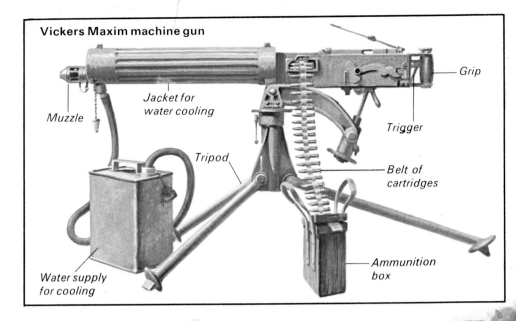

Vickers Maxim machine gun

Muzzle

Jacket for water cooling

Tripod

Water supply for cooling

Grip

Trigger

Belt of cartridges

Ammunition box

▼ Large attacks usually began with very heavy shelling intended to smash the barbed wire and give the attackers a clear path. When the barrage stopped the infantry would go over the top and cross "no man's land". Few attacks were really successful and casualties were enormous. There were often smaller raids to capture prisoners and obtain information.

The modern soldier

A changing role

Over the last century there has been a gradual change in the soldier's job. For centuries all he had to do was obey orders without question. He knew very little beyond how to handle his weapons. Since the middle of the 19th century science has given the soldier more and more new equipment. The new soldier has had to become more of an expert and ready to think for himself.

During World War I he learned to drive cars and tanks, to fly, operate the radio and complicated machinery. He had to act as a member of a team as well as on his own. This was even more true during World War II (1939-45) and is still the case today.

Much of the work that a modern soldier does today has little to do with large wars. His time may be spent fighting against people of his own country who disagree with the government. He is also called upon to keep the peace between groups who disagree. In many ways he has become a kind of policeman.

New equipment

The gay, glamorous uniforms of the past have gone except for ceremonial occasions. Dull, practical overalls that blend in with the background are worn by most troops today. The head is protected by some form of metal or plastic helmet with a padded lining.

In some danger areas many of the troops wear some kind of protective garment. These are often called "flak jackets" and they will stop bomb splinters and most low-powered bullets. New plastics and metals are used in the construction of these jackets.

Most of the world's infantry now carry an automatic rifle firing a small calibre bullet, whilst officers carry an automatic pistol. There are many specialized weapons such as anti-tank missiles, radar search equipment and infra-red sights, which enable the user to see in the dark.

For his police work, the soldier uses blast grenades which stun but do not kill and chemical gases which discomfort but do not injure. He has a special "riot" uniform which will not tear and carries a face guard and a large plastic or metal shield to ward off stones or other missiles.

▶ These American troops were involved in fighting in the jungles of Vietnam. It was a very specialized type of warfare for which the Americans used the newest developments in chemical and mechanical equipment.

▼ During times of unrest, crowds can become so great that the police are not strong enough to control them. The army is often called in to help. Troops are also called in when any important service breaks down.

◀ U.N. troops in the Middle East. The United Nations was set up to settle quarrels between states. Several countries lend troops to the United Nations to act as peacemakers and prevent further fighting.

A modern soldier and his equipment

▶ Soldiers from all over the world now look very similar. This figure is dressed in a mixture of equipment from different countries.
His helmet is the U.S. pattern with a plastic inner part and a steel outside. His tough, waterproof boots are also American and the straps to carry his equipment are of the British pattern.

▶ He wears a camouflage jacket of the French pattern to blend into the background. His weapon is a fine Russian assault rifle, AK 47. This will fire 7.62 mm. bullets at a rate of 400 rounds a minute.

▲ British respirators
Chemical warfare has not been used on a large scale since 1914-18, but tear gas is often used in riots. These respirators filter out gas.

▲ British anti-riot equipment
In riots the greatest danger is from stones and bottles not bullets. Strong plastic shields protect the troops. They may use wooden sticks.

▲ Soviet RPG 7 anti-tank missile
This missile is fired from a tube held on the shoulder. It has a rocket motor which starts after it leaves the tube. Fins steady it in flight. It can penetrate 320 mm. of armour.

◀ Soviet FI grenade
The pin is pulled out, the lever released and it explodes after about 4 seconds with great effect.

▶ Israel UZI sub machine gun
A light, simple weapon used by many countries as well as Israel. It fires 9 mm. bullets at a rate of 600 rounds a minute.

Projects make your own arms and armour

How to make Roman armour

You will need some thin card, newspaper, glue, paste, paper clips and scissors.

The helmet

Cut four or five long strips of card about 38 mm. wide. Take one, encircle your head and secure the ends. Put this one on and take a second strip. Pass it under the band on the side of your head, over the top of your head and under the band on the other side. Then fix it in place and trim off any spare ends. Repeat this with a strip going from the front to the back of the head. Run a couple of other strips across the head at angles. You now have a framework for the helmet.

Tear up some newspaper into long, narrow strips and thoroughly paste one, then carefully smooth it over the framework. Work your way round carefully smoothing the strips and overlapping the pieces until you have completely covered the helmet. Set it aside to dry and then repeat twice more. By this time you should have a light but tough bowl for the helmet. Leave it to dry completely.

Place the bowl on a sheet of card and trace round the back to obtain its shape. Draw a fairly wide peak shape and on the inside of your "shape" line draw another line about 25 mm. away. Cut out the whole shape and then make a series of cuts about 25 mm. apart and going up to your shape line. Bend up the tabs you have made. Put glue on the side facing the peak and carefully stick them on the inside of your helmet at the back.

You can do the same at the front. This peak should be smaller and set above the rim. Cut out two fairly large ear flaps to reach down to the chin and glue these in place. When dry, paint the helmet bronze or silver.

How to make a Roman helmet

Card

Pasted paper strips

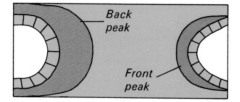

Back peak

Front peak

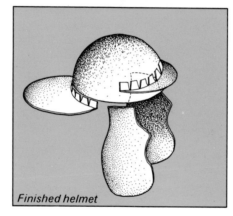

Finished helmet

▲ This modern copy shows exactly what a Roman armour, or *lorica segmentata* of the first century A.D. would have looked like. It is made of steel with bronze trimmings. Paint or spray your finished model silver and bronze and draw lines across the body armour to represent the sections.

Roman body armour

Measure a piece of card wide enough to reach from the armpit to the waist and long enough to go round your body and overlap at the front. Use paperclips to fasten it as they are easy to undo when you want to take it off. You need two strips to go over the shoulder. They should be rectangular with an extra piece at the centre where they cross over the shoulder. You will need a little help to position these two strips and they should cross the shoulders at a slight angle. Secure at the back with glue but use paper clips for the front. From the waist belt hang a number of strips covered with metal scales. These can be made from lengths of tape and squares of card.

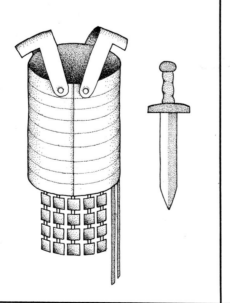

A Roman shield

To make the shield you will need a large piece of card which is slightly curved. If you cannot find a large enough piece you could make one with several sheets of newspaper well pasted together. It needs to be long enough to reach from your waist to the ground. Fix a couple of strips inside so that you can hold it. On the front paint a design or pattern.

Roman weapons

Look at the illustration on page 8 to see the shape of a Roman sword. It is probably easier to cut one from thick card, but if you want a strong weapon you could use a fretsaw and plywood. Make the sheath from folded card and decorate it.

Make a mediaeval castle

You will need card, plastic bottles, toilet roll tubes, scissors and glue. It is important to know the size of the model soldiers you will be using so that you can work out the size of the castle.

Make the walls out of card and fit a walk along the top. If you use card it should be carefully folded and stuck in position. Leave enough space above the walk so that a figure, when on the wall, is guarded by the wall. Cut slits to make the battlements.

Towers and a keep

Make the towers from plastic bottles and cardboard tubes. If you use plastic bottles you will need to cut off the necks before cutting the battlements. Join the towers to the walls with glue (you may need a special glue to stick the plastic) or with sticky tape.

Most castles had one large, extra strong tower known as the keep which was inside the walls. Make this from a suitable box and fit some towers on the corners. Square towers can be made by folding card into a square tube with a tab to join the edges.

Decide on the position of the gate and draw a door shape in the wall. Cut along the centre line and round the top as far as A and you can open and close the doors.

The drawbridge

The drawbridge is simply a piece of card of the right size. At one end there is a tab which can be used as the hinge and should be secured to the base of the wall under the gate. You will need to shape the tab.

Just above the door and near the sides, pierce two holes in the wall. Pass thin string or thread through these and tie them to the end of the bridge. You can now raise and lower your bridge. If the bridge proves awkward and will not lower you may need some extra weight. Add a strip of plasticine along the front edge.

Siege weapons

The illustration of the 14th century siege on pages 12-13 might give you ideas for making siege weapons. These can be made from lollipop sticks, balsa wood, elastic bands and matchsticks. The siege tower can be made from a square tube of card with a simple drawbridge at the top.

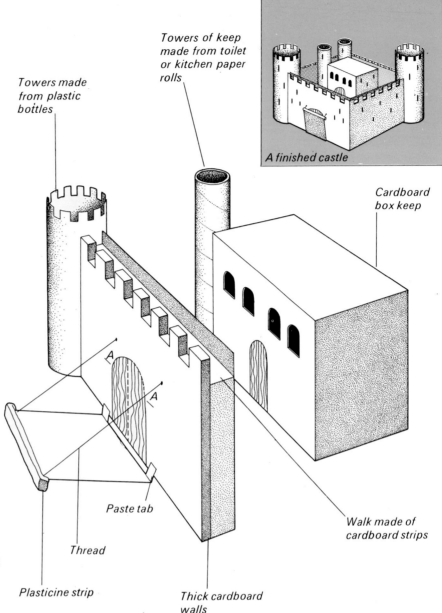

Towers of keep made from toilet or kitchen paper rolls

A finished castle

Towers made from plastic bottles

Cardboard box keep

A

A

Walk made of cardboard strips

Paste tab

Thread

Plasticine strip

Thick cardboard walls

Make your own model revolver

Find a picture of the revolver you want to copy, which must be a side view. The picture will probably be much too small to copy so you must enlarge it.

Take a piece of tracing paper and draw a rectangle big enough to cover the picture. Divide it into small squares. Take your plywood and draw a rectangle on it. The size of the rectangle will depend on the size of the picture you want to copy. If the picture is 130 mm. long and you want to make your model 390 mm. long, the rectangle must be three times as big and each square must be three times as big. Now copy the shape in the picture rectangle on to the corresponding square of the copy rectangle. Cut out the finished copy with a fretsaw.

If you want a cylinder in the revolver, use a cotton reel. Cut out a space slightly smaller than the reel so that it fits tightly.

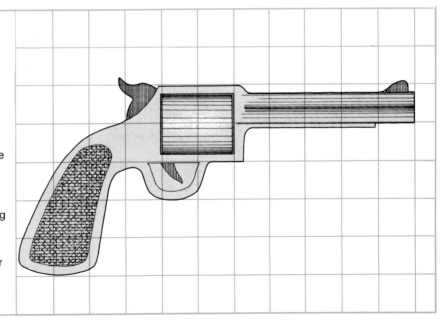

Reference and glossary

What to do next

Many museums in Britain have good collections of arms and armour. The largest collections may be seen at the following museums:

London
The Tower of London
Victoria & Albert Museum
Imperial War Museum
The Wallace Collection
National Army Museum
York
Castle Museum
Lincoln
City and County Museum
Newcastle
Laing Art Gallery & Museum
John G. Joicey Museum
The Keep Museum
Museum of Antiquities
Birmingham
City Museum and Art Gallery
Cambridge
Fitzwilliam Museum
Canterbury
The Westgate
Chester
Grosvenor Museum
Maidstone
Museum and Art Gallery
Oxford
The Pitt Rivers Museum
Edinburgh
National Museum of Antiquities
of Scotland
Royal Scottish Museum
Glasgow
Art Gallery & Museum
Old Glasgow Museum

There are many smaller regimental museums in many of the towns of England and Wales. You can find details of these at your local public library.

Model soldiers
You can find out a great deal about uniforms and weapons by collecting model soldiers. You can buy them unpainted from 30p to £7.00 each and learn a lot by finding out details of the uniforms and weapons and painting them. There are several model soldier societies and shops which specialize in them.

Glossary

arming doublet a padded garment with mail patches to protect danger points.

backplate armour for the back of the body.

bolt short arrow for a crossbow.

brass a brass slab placed over a tomb and cut with the likeness of the person buried beneath it.

breastplate armour for the chest.

bullet the part of a cartridge fired out of a gun.

cartridge the paper or metal container holding bullet, powder and a cap and used to load a firearm.

coif mail hood to cover head and neck.

cranequin geared device for spanning or winding back string of crossbow.

flintlock the mechanism designed to produce sparks by striking flint to steel.

fulminate a chemical which explodes when struck a blow.

gunpowder a mixture of sulphur, saltpetre and charcoal making a dangerous explosive.

joust a combat between two people.

lames strips of metal making up a piece of armour.

lance a long spear carried by horsemen.

legion a unit of the Roman army.

mail a construction of metal rings forming a mesh or net which was a very good form of defence.

melée a fight in which any number of people took part.

mine a tunnel dug under a wall or fortification.

musket a firearm with a long, smooth barrel which fires a ball.

percussion cap a small copper cap containing a tiny amount of fulminate.

phalanx a large formation of men armed with long spears.

priming fine gunpowder placed in the pan next to the touch hole and fired by the sparks from the lock.

quarrel arrow from a crossbow.

squire a knight's personal assistant whose job it was to help dress and take care of him.

tilt a joust which is held with a wooden fence separating the horses.

trebuchet a siege engine; a catapult worked by a heavy weight.

wheellock the mechanical system using a steel wheel and a piece of pyrites to strike sparks from a weapon.

Books to read

A Knight and his Armour. A Knight and his Horse. A Knight and his Weapons. A Knight and his Castle. All by R.E. Oakeshott (Lutterworth Press)

Let's Look at Arms and Armour by Frederick Wilkinson (Frederick Muller 1968)

Arms and Armour by Vesey Norman (Weidenfeld & Nicolson 1964)

Warrior to Soldier 449-1660 by A.V.B. Norman and D. Pottinger (Weidenfeld & Nicolson 1966)

Guns by Dudley Pope (Hamlyn 1969)

Sporting Guns by Richard Akehurst (Weidenfeld & Nicolson 1968)

Spotlight on Soldiers by Frederick Wilkinson (Hamlyn 1973)

Index

Illustration Credits

Key to the positions of illustrations: (T) top, (C) centre, (B) bottom.

Artists:
Angus McBride/Faulkner-Marks Group; 3, 4-5
Peter Connolly: 6-7
Sackett Publishing Services Ltd.: 8-9, 18-19
W. Francis Phillips: 10-11, 24-5
Peter North: 12-13, 30-1, 32-3
Dan Escott: 14-15
Chris Forsey: 16-17, 22-3, 34-5, 36-7
Ron Hayward: 20-1
Brian Lebrani/Zip Art: 26-7
Michael Youens/Sackett Publishing Services Ltd.: 28-9

Malcolm McGregor: 38-9, 43
Edward Mortelmans/John Martin & Artists Ltd.: 40-1
Ray Burrows and Corinne Clarke: 44-5

Photographs
Author's collection: 17 (Victoria & Albert Museum), 25, 32, 44
British Museum/John Freeman: 26
Christ's College: 22
Giraudon: 30
Michael Holford: 28
Keystone Press: 42 (C)
Mansell Collection: 11
Popperfoto: 42 (T)
United Nations: 42 (B)